SINGULARITIES

poems by

David T. Manning

Finishing Line Press
Georgetown, Kentucky

SINGULARITIES

These poems are for my wife Doris, for her unending love and patience with a poet husband.

Also a special thanks to Carol Peters for her helpful suggestions on so many of my poems over the years.

Copyright © 2018 by David T. Manning
ISBN 978-1-63534-533-9 First Edition
All rights reserved under International and Pan-American Copyright Conventions. No part of this book may be reproduced in any manner whatsoever without written permission from the publisher, except in the case of brief quotations embodied in critical articles and reviews.

ACKNOWLEDGMENTS

I would like to thank the following sources for their publication of individual poems, sometimes in slightly different versions or with different titles:

Bay Leaves: "[Exit Pettigrew]"
Cider Press Review: "An Outdoor Wedding"
Iodine Poetry Journal: "Fat Crow"
KaKaLaK, 2008 Anthology of Carolina Poets: "The Forever Poem"
KaKaLaK 2017 Anthology of Carolina Poets: "Thin Air"
Looking Back, A Poetry and Prose Anthology, (Old Mountain Press, 2007): "Moment Musicale"
Main Street Rag: "At The Holiday Inn Parking Lot," "The Church Youth Group," "Higher Learning," "I Have These Damn Dreams," "The Medium," "No Country for Old Men," "On Citizenship," "Patent Pending," "Poet's Lunch," "Quantum Logic for Everyman," "Singularities," and "Twenty-One Grams of Soul"
Mythic Delirium: "The Next Station"
Potato Eyes: "Preacher Ramey's Baptism"

"Around the Campfire" and "At the Neighborhood Homeowners' Meeting" first appeared in Detained by the Authorities by David Treadway Manning (Pudding House Publications, 2007)

Publisher: Leah Maines
Editor: Christen Kincaid
Cover Art: The Library of Congress and is The Wessyngton Water Tower of Cedar Hill, Robertson County, Tennessee
Author Photo: Ellen Giamportone
Cover Design: Elizabeth Maines McCleavy

Printed in the USA on acid-free paper.
Order online: www.finishinglinepress.com
also available on amazon.com

Author inquiries and mail orders:
Finishing Line Press
P. O. Box 1626
Georgetown, Kentucky 40324
U. S. A.

Table of Contents

The Church Youth Group 1
An Outdoor Wedding 2
Ten-Thirty Mass 3
Remembering Doreen 4
Preacher Ramey's Baptism 5
One More Final Reunion 6
Higher Learning 7
At The Holiday Inn Parking Lot 8
Quantum Logic for Everyman 9
Twenty-One Grams of Soul 10
The Medium 11
Summer North 12
The Next Station 13
Keep Moving 14
Happy New Year! 15
Moment Musicale 16
The Audition 17
At the Neighborhood Homeowners' Meeting 19
Around the Campfire 20
The Board Meeting 21
Patent Pending 22
Fat Crow 23
Miserere Nobis 24
Poet's Lunch 25
On Citizenship 26
I have these damn dreams 27
Of Mack and Rena 28
No Country for Old Men 29
The Best is Yet to Be 30
[Exit Pettigrew] 31
Singularities 32
Travelling 33
Thin Air 34
The Forever Poem 35

The Church Youth Group

Circa 1940

The Church, First Holy Majesty, in Los Angeles
had a huge choir, for which we stood at attention
like the Star Spangled Banner as they marched in.
Their tall handsome minister fought Communism
& passed out "Freedom Kits" to the faithful so his flock
could detect socialist thought, and not be sheared
of their goods. Preacher lived in Golden Harbour
        & had lots of wool.

They sprinkled me into salvation! That done
I was assimilated into churchlife with a young-folks
roller skating party in the church's cavernous gymnasium.
Think of it—hundreds of bright-young-smiling-faces
flying round & round, their steel wheels roaring
like thunder as they swayed and swung
        like fools on Benzedrine.

I had never learned to roller-skate & should have left
but sat it all out alone in another room—where
I went through my billfold for an hour or so.
I am happy to report the party was a huge success
& their Freedom Kits detected no subversive infiltration.

An Outdoor Wedding

When the Sacred Heart Church caught fire
the wedding was moved to the parish garden
under the smoking olive trees
where the bride's and groom's families
waited, toasting marshmallows over the blaze.
The big red diocesan fire truck showed up
and Kevin O'Connor and Marco Salvino
pumped secular water onto the inferno,
flames leaping from the vats of holy oil
and other spirits set alight.

Arriving late to the wedding
I relieved myself in the parish house restroom,
lost in an old-growth forest
of priests lined up at urinals,
their lemony streams turning pinot noir
from the transubstantiation there.

It was a wedding to remember.
Everyone said there had been
a miracle, for the new wine wasn't
watery at all. The assembled clergy,
vestments sweaty from the pep rally for Saint
Jodocus, patron against fire, and wearied
from the massive miracle performed,
held the new couple to be especially blessed,
and the wine a full-bodied noir,
rivaling the best outputs of all the friars of France.

Ten-Thirty Mass

Four rows back from Father
he considers the homily on the future

state of souls. Gunner's gaze
behind black shades, he never moves

his long straight helmet mouth
(with its rumor of a smile). Cords

of his neck sink like an oak—down
into his brown shirt collar, grounded

in private doubts, level clamp of lips
weary of arguments waged encyclicals ago.

Remembering Doreen

Doreen Rafferty—how could I forget
the name, her red hair, her eyes, green
as Dublin in the Spring. It was her birthday!
There was a cake and someone playing
"Kerry Dancers" and "Mavourneen"
on an old piano. Some were dancing
reels in hard-soled Irish shoes. It was late
at night in an apartment somewhere
off California Highway 101.

But it was Doreen—the name—
that made me want to love her
and I would have swapped my date for her
but I was young and thought her legs—
or was it her teeth?—were less than perfect,
distorted as I was by Hollywood.

Dear God! Sitting here a continent away
that name comes back
over so much time. I wish her
perfection in all her necessary parts.
I wish her everlasting life, and hope
her portrait hangs high in the halls of Carlow
and that all the little leprechauns
will leap for her. And that her name
will never be given again.

Preacher Ramey's Baptism

Preacher Ramey saved four-hundred
souls from Hell that night,
four-hundred scared to Jesus, but
little Billy Samuels who asked
if he could have a night-light
in the everlasting and was told No
sobbed himself home. I followed Preacher

from the tent when he left
that anguished boy—
followed with my heavy Bible.
And when the two of us crossed
Johnson's Creek, thinking of Billy,
I brought that black Book down on him
with both hands, sent Ramey to his knees
and with the provided stones and water
quenched his hellfire palaver.

Johnson's Creek runs swift and cold
and to that poor Jordan I fed
our Sunday man, peaceful now,
baptized against the deep cold stones.
Baptized to last, I hope.

One More Final Reunion

When the storm came ashore
in San Pedro harbor Aunt Jo's house
guests, with their martinis, got caught out
in it under the Brazilian Pepper trees
so they all crowded into her potting shed
until she led them to shelter,
lighting their way with a jar of fireflies.
      In the old house lights flash
on and off, room to room
like traffic signals in the dark.
Family pictures, Uncle Omar,
Aunt Callie, long gone, are back
from Indiana, with good solid
viewpoints of the nineteen-thirties,
slow dancing in the windy hallway.
One by one, old school friends show up
for one more reunion. They whisper
in the drafty chart-room.
          Wow! My old teachers are back!
Mrs. Fisher from Geometry,
the nice Communist with her gigantic
black poodle; Mr. Walker from Physics
charging up his Leyden Jars;
Mr. Hammock, the pyrotechnic chemist,
still bandaged, hands stained
with permanganate, all back
for final guest appearances.
Their frail selves are of the finest silk,
lighted gossamer afloat
in the wind.

Higher Learning

> *Montebello, California, 1943*

The word was
the red raiders would
meet us under
the Bella Vista water tower
at 10:00 that night
to settle things, so
all day in Mr. Ratchitt's
9th grade metal shop

we made knucks
of cold rolled steel
leaving the edges
burred. But somebody
tipped the cops
and that night, ten or so
showed up in squad cars
with blue spotlights,
along with a few parents

and a church camp
councilor with bibles
and a stack of pamphlets
on healthy activities
for the young.
And that was that.

At the Holiday Inn Parking Lot

Land of the Brave

100,000 square feet of concrete.
8a.m. & 90 in the shade
3 Ford Expeditions, 5 Navigators,

One empty Peterbilt panting
blue exhaust, across
12 parking spaces. One

Tennessee family in cargo shorts,
shrieking kids corralled
from elevator tag.

Dad's shirt sweat-stuck to his back,
shirt back stuck to the car seat.

Behind dad's seat, kids plus 2 rubber
dinosaurs, a plastic kangaroo and
one kid with loaded diapers.

God bless America!
On with the vacation!

Quantum Logic for Everyman

Consensus holds that Einstein went
too far, trying to build a logic edifice for
the quantum world, a bridge of reason

spanning subatomic realms and our domain
of cats and chairs and men. In Copenhagen,
Bohr knew isotopes popped off alpha, beta,

gamma shots like random champagne
corks of plastered revelers and reasoned,
there is no reason in that tiny world,

nor cause to look for any. *Stuff happens*
would rightly state his view. Einstein
went to his grave still seeking causes

for things, large or small. I think Albert
was right. Still, as I jog this dark dawn road
cars pass, now two, now twenty

in a string, then none, pattern-less
as atoms in a gas. Einstein might deduce
a cause, but I see none. I think of a vast

observer, feet on separate planets,
viewing us from an ecliptic stance,
how he might see this filament of road,

cars like quarks impelled by schemes
unknown and decide our world
is run by stoned fraternity boys.

Twenty-One Grams of Soul

> SOUL HAS WEIGHT, PHYSICIAN THINKS.
> *Dr. MacDougall of Haverhill Tells of Experiments at Death.*
> —New York Times, 1901

Accused of sorcery, Leonardo
dissected for it,
finding meat.

It must be tiny—if at all—
in its putative pineal seat. But look
how Everything began
ex nihilo, Aquinas said.

Like Leonardo, materially inclined,
MacDougall weighed *something* that escaped
a man, dying on a grocer's scale. Attempts
to replicate gave mixed results. Yet physics
does not forbid a living energy
the God particle can barely feel. Again,

think small: Subnano gall midge. Hips
of a quark (How many Plancks in a quark?).
Is your soul *You*—all of *you* tucked
between the orbitals of lithium?
Planck-length inkdot that could paint
the Matterhorn with stain to spare?

Suppose cats and even marigolds have souls.
When their bodies fail, whatever's
weightless runs the ship's rat-rope
from dying. Later, ghosts of the ages
fill and swell the space between the stars.

The Medium

Most of them know
I'm a fake, but they don't
believe either.
They come for the show.
We all know no one
answers the door over there.
So I take their money
and give them a little smoke
and a few faint
Miles Davis licks.

OK, a few old ones believe,
but they don't have that long
anyway. They don't get hurt—
I'm a grief therapist for God's sake!
What the hell, we're all in denial
about this.
          This crazy business!
Every now and then someone
brings a flashlight. And once
I had to tell a lady "please,
no cell phones for the dead."

But the mother who came
in yesterday, whose little girl
went over a hill on her trike—
I didn't have anything for that…

This lousy damn business.
What do I know about anything?
I'd like to be wrong
about nobody over there.
I'd like to be surprised.

Summer North

When the poles reversed, the sea horse
latitudes drifted north, Greenland melted,
Orion fell from the sky. In Labrador,

white Rigel's fire lit the dogwoods
at Pentecost. Now, at forty north, summer
buries us in snow. It's late May

and the ground is numb, no land can
sleep in this wind. I search dead stems
for buds. Only wild onions wave

dark sprouts from vacant lots. Raw
weather sucks the house's heat. Wind
leaks into sleep. Tonight, O dream—

hunt me up a June storm. Let me hunker
in stream-side caves with gusty fires.
Tomorrow, sirocco—fly me to the green island.

The Next Station

Riding the 7:05 uptown,
a new conductor
stopped by my seat.

He wore a strange uniform,
dark blue, all covered with stars.

I thought maybe he was advertising
Michelin or Pepsi like
a Nascar dude, but

the stars made pictures—
with names like *Orion, Cetus,*
the *Southern Cross.*

Outside, it was getting dark.
"What's all this?" I asked.

"Who knows what *your* plans
were?," he said. "I'm here to tell you
about the next station."

Keep Moving

I've hung around too long
made you all grow old
while I didn't age at all. You see
I catalyze progeria.
With your lives in my hands
I betrayed you.
In my defense I can only say
your aging was imperceptible.
I couldn't see what I was
doing. I have my own file—
read only—on all of you
where you never change.
And you wouldn't have changed
if I hadn't hung around too long.
I couldn't see my own doing
until I came back for
that 25th reunion. My God,
what I did to you!
Now I must move on
to where people are young
enough to resist me
for awhile
and keep on moving.

Happy New Year!

The people stand and cheer
the new year in. The TV screens
all show Times Square at midnight as

the great glittering ball descends
from God Himself, back in His Heaven
forgiving the ruined past, absolving us

of the mess we made of Paradise.
All the TV screens agree this is a
Beginning Beyond Our Dreams.

The bands and bright parades mean
Great Things are coming. Get on board!
Join hands! The crowds cheer

as their momentum flushes them
into 2018 and everyone gets wrecked
on the bubbly illusion of control.

Moment Musicale

> *For the Charleston Civic Chorus,*
> *Charleston, West Virginia*

Rewinding time to some realm
lost in universes past
Authur Drake, recording expert,
has not yet accidentally erased
my *Three Sundays of a Poet* tape.

                          He shuffles
into the choir room
with his standard fifty dollars
of loose change ajingle, but who can tell
because we're practicing
Stravinsky's *Symphony of Psalms*
which even when sung right

                          sounds wrong
(though who can tell
because we never sang it right).
And I could look through all
past universes, find the same.

But right now Drake is safely
silver-weighted to his chair,
my tape will live another hour
(I think I'll rest right here).

The Audition

What was I thinking,
singing *Walther's Prize Song*
from Die Meistersinger
to an audience of critics
and musicians?

Margaret Hope, my teacher,
said, "You can do it!"
Lovely Sally Ann who played
for me was all decked out
and so fresh in white with pink
polka-dots. (I think she likes me too).

And I was armed with the vast
bad judgment of the young,
who stare down windmills,
stand off armies of the night,
and know he was master of that song!

So what was I thinking,
auditioning with an aria from Wagner's
opera, for the symphony, in that room
of real musicians, serious students
advanced in preparing for careers?

And Geoffrey, the scowling conductor
of the symphony, was there to enforce
strict time with a nickel-plated
whistle for police which he blew
when I still had one-half page to go.

The judges cleared their throats.
Noting my need for better tone support,
they all agreed my German diction
was good—almost that of a real singer
of that song.

The winner, all in her gown
of white, sang "Un Bel Di" from
Madama Butterfly, while I was
shattered, reduced to black
quarter-notes smoldering in a pile.

Sally, in her rose pink and white,
never spoke to me again and married
an acned red-haired boy
who couldn't sing.

Years later I think of the boy in me
of such reckless courage
and wonder who he was,
so certain he could sing.

**At the Neighborhood
Homeowners' Meeting**

last night, I noticed you
in your PTA wire-rims and
concerned-citizen tie. As I listened

carefully to your remarks,
your portrait—*shit-head*—bloomed
before me like a Polaroid.

As you continued our enlightenment,
considering scenarios A, B, and C
I thought upon death

and life, and values blown
and the Giants-Cubs game I was
missing, and felt a sense of shame

for such judgment of another
who should be born again
with sufficient oxygen.

Around the Campfire

The MFAs were camping out under the stars, trying to keep a small fire going. They looked pale and unhealthy in the moonlight. I walked up, uninvited, and sat down. After a while, one of them read a post-modern sonnet, and the next one, a post-structuralist villanelle, which the others had memorized because they all joined in, chanting the final stanza. There was a period of silence, then a flurry of talk about the impact of post-deconsructionist minimalism upon the New York School. Then it was my turn. The magic of the moon and the night was upon me and I read my prize-winning *Rondeau for Air-Pump and Teakwood Hammers*. There was a long silence, then the apparent leader of the group spoke. "That showed some elements of literacy," he said.

The Board Meeting

I have a message that badly
needs saying (it will change
the world!)

Everything the two sides
are arguing
can be reconciled
by one simple statement!

So I wait
for a lull in the salvos
of cross-talk as it rolls
like a molten ball of gold
behind my eyes,

like the charge in a cocked '44 waits
for a nervous finger. BANG! And off
she goes, brain rolling in an idiot dream,
an avalanching luge of runaway words,
no hope of changing a one.

I hear a stranger, some fool
babbling in an echo chamber, my God, it's me!
too late, did I say that? Did I say it
anywhere near right?
What will the damn minutes say?

Patent Pending

"Roshi"
mechanical Zenmaster brings
a touch of Kyoto to our county fair.

Approach his mat & drop a quarter
in his slot & bow. He bows, then
pitches koans like batting practice

balls—right at you to blow
your head away. At the end
you get to ask one question

& get it right first time! If you ask
"what is truth?"
Joyously, he will attack you

from his small iron heart
raining kicks & blows
teaching the truth of pain.

Fat Crow

Never such strong opinions
from so spare a perch
but this loud crow, black
as only the devil, or Luther's
thrown inkwell must have his say
from the topmost twig.

Too big for the pine stem
he yaws in the breeze like a fat drunk.
Each gust makes this inkblot sumo
lurch and flap to keep from toppling back.
This idiot is alive, but, above all,

black! Black bill, black eyes.
So big and rowdy black
so Menckenesque to come
from just an egg.
A human so assured I'd smash
but not this glossy clown.

Miserere Nobis

At 4:00 am I woke from
phoning up dead people in the night.

Some of them
were at home.
They sounded
worn out.
We chatted briefly.
All their news was old.

From a dim room,
Benny Goodman's clarinet:
a lone senior waltzing to
In the Mood,
dragging toilet paper
on his shoe.

I got up and fell
asleep making coffee.
What a life.

Poet's Lunch

The shrimp, red-curried,
look up at me

from their tiny souls
with their red-curried eyes,

still haunt me
as I take my pill,

walk down the driveway
to rejection.

My blood pressure
is in the mailbox.

On Citizenship

Should I have
reported
the gigantic rat

greasy and gray
with bristling whiskers
scuttling
under the shelves
of Fancy Feast cat food

to the check-out
lady
in Lowe's Grocery
today?

I have these damn dreams

of dark places,
old mansions or warehouses
with hundreds of rooms and
thousands of light-switches,
none of which work, and

high up in the cobwebs
is a gigantic porcelain knob which
I heave on until it cranks

to scenes of dear friends
doing things
I won't tell you about. Then
I'm skipping down a slope
of poppies in the Ojai Valley
and the hill becomes
the Chrysler Building.

But the best is when
I'm the tenor soloist
in Verdi's Requiem
and arrive at the theater
at up-beat of the baton
with no score
and no light if I had one.

Of Mack & Rena

1954, think of it, sixteen typists
at MagnaChem picked for good legs
and smarts with their IBM Selectrics.
Like fillies lined up in their stalls,
the typing pool, Job One—to please
one horny boss, i.e.

      Mack Scranie, hair, black
buzz-cut, Levis low and tight,
knew his way around his chicks.
Funny Mack who made us laugh
telling about his naughty wife.
About to spank her for a rumpled
shirt he lost it at the sight of her
cute bottom, round and white
& took her for a cuddled bounce
on their Seely innerspring.

      All this meant zilch to pool typist
Rena Crall, red hair, rawboned & tall
to whom fell Scranie's Monthly
to type up. Rena, of the strict style
manual school, took no lip from horny
bosses & itchy office-boys. Scranie
bunched up into BigBosshood
when his work came back from Rena
decorated like an Easter egg,
his fourth-grade capitals
blue-penciled out. When Rena
balked at butchering the prose
of Jefferson, BigBoss Scranie bounced
      her out. So Rena

with her good grammer, spunk
& one autistic six-year-old boy
followed the ads for "positions wanted,"
secretaries with "people skills" &
a "vision proper for
a smoothly-working team."

No Country for Old Men

Once before his gentling
by age and failed plumbing
he lusted after women

in tiny black dresses
who crossed mysterious legs
in whispering flesh-toned hose.

As discretely as he could
with mirrors on his loafers
he looked up their skirts

till one day on a windy field
the soccer girls came running
with piston legs pumping

under long thick woolen socks
over calves with rawhide cords.
They could run and kick forever

and neuter a man with a header.
And in his vision he saw how
they sweat, how they would shower,

comb and put on White Shoulders
(those girls with whipcord sinews
under their tiny black dresses)

and how he'd been attracted
to an ambush of kicks and muscles
to kill him, at least dismember

those loving parts he remembered
(all this while running and laughing).
How could he have been so wrong?

The Best Is Yet to Be

with apologies to Robert Browning

I have reached the age
when I can get away with things!
        But I'm still young.
Must I project an aura of senilty—
flannel, Vics and Musterole?
I am most free in darkness.
I must watch myself when dressed for decency;
weddings, a christening, the party scene. A laughing
grandfather with some rumors
of a giddy past. Old folks! Who would not
overlook a rich bump here, a nuzzle there?
And when the party's done, few men
my age are jailed for such small joys,
so little remembered from the dizziness
of champagne. Who but the vilest lecher
would disguise his delicious plunder
as a grandfatherly squeeze? So young friends
"Grow old along with me!" The downward
glide should be through fields Elysian.
And when my gaze flows upward
from your knees take comfort, join my
communion, knowing only how
I admire the harmony of your skirt's
soft shade, blush peach against
the recliner where you curl so charmingly.

[Exit Pettigrew]

> "...before the disappearance of Ambrose Small,
> Ambrose Bierce had disappeared...Was
> somebody collecting Ambroses?"
> —*The Books of Charles Fort*

When Mr. Pettigrew fell down
in his Petunia bed & died
he left the water faucet on
but no one rallied to his side

until, at length, the street became
a busy stream. The neighbors knew
an old man's folly was to blame
& went to chasten Pettigrew.

Why must the young consign the old
to fuddy-dom? Someday they'll rue
the condescension when they're told
"We only want what's best for you."

> They turned it off, then looked around:
> they searched the woods beyond the lawn,
> the house, the trees, the flowered ground.
> But Mr. Pettigrew was gone.

Singularities

Behind the canned-corn shelf
at Lowe's Grocery, a thin spot in the wall
is all that's between us and a wormhole
in the universe.
Few know of this.
But luckless Irma Groat, who fell, reaching
for a can of golden bantam, chanced
to brush against the tiny forbidden spot
and now circles, timeless, beyond the tail-star
of the Great Bear. These singularities
are commoner than most realize!
Dead spots in spacetime are everywhere.

At Sixth and Concord
of my town there's a knot hole
in the ballpark fence where,
any Saturday afternoon, one can see
Roger Maris' mighty swing
ripping number sixty-one
over and over again. (O faithful—
let us raise our voices and someday
he may yet make Cooperstown!)
Get a good left-field seat with
an outfielder's glove.
Balls seldom make it to the street.

So look just behind the canned-corn
next to Heinz's beans where
these riches flourish out-of-sight.
Take note! Sometimes some lucky
Mickey Mantle fan just disappears.

Travelling

You ask me about
the next crossing, the one
after the boulders, road
washed out,
narrow switchback over

    a creekbed
above the falls
two thousand feet down
and already I am
against the wall
with your questions.

What can I tell you?
My bones are like
    your bones.

But if you can make
magic from what I say,
take it.

We give life
to each other,
travelling.

Thin Air

Just past Wilson's Cienega
hiking the San Jacinto trail
a Haiku came down
from the blue ozone sky
so I wrote it out in my mind
scrambling around rock slides
through scrub pines and oak
just over 10,000 feet
as I looked down
to where I once got lost
a whole day in sunlit Long Valley
then far into the gray forever
the poem safe inside.
      I kept on past trail springs,
through Manzanita, blackjack oak,
chinquapin, wild water bubbling up
everywhere, sun hot in the thin air
past dark granite walls
with sparkling mica changing
sun colors in the high blue.
Up at the summit
there was a tin can
with a tiny spiral booklet,
a pencil tied to it
previously signed by "Sky-High Joe"
      who said (in 1994)
You must be drunk or stupid to be here.
Joe left a space below for my Haiku, but
it was gone, every word gone
somewhere back down the trail
waiting for some lucky poet to find.

The Forever Poem

Again it's light—
an unspoiled day.
All the bad choices,
the sins
have not yet kicked in.

The world seems to be running
smoothly without me.
The morning paper has not yet
arrived to tell me
what to be upset about.
The flicker happily drums
the rain gutter without my instructions.

All praise
to the rumbling forced-air furnace,
the coffee maker (burbling to life)
to the growling stomach
of my cat (black velvet nose
prodding me for tuna).
All praise to self-reliant miracles
everywhere, spared in these early
moments of befuddlement,
from my stupendous power
to screw them up.

Soon, I will thrust my hand back into
the watch-works of creation,
gum up a dozen wonders—
but for now, a determined ant
trudges the ceiling above me.
Tomorrow will come, and once more
the world will wait for me
to sleep
so it can heal.

David Treadway Manning is a Pushcart nominee and three-time winner of the North Carolina Poetry Society's Poet Laureate Award. His poems have appeared in *Southern Poetry Review, Tar River Poetry, Rattle, 32 Poems* and other journals and is included in *Literary Trails of Eastern North Carolina, a Guidebook* (Georgann Eubanks). He is a past winner of the Longleaf Chapbook competition and *Crucible* magazine's Sam Ragan Award. He has nine chapbooks, most recently *The Girl Who Came Out with the Stars* (Old Mountain Press, 2012) and *Genes* (Finishing Line, 2013). Previous full-length collections are *The Flower Sermon* (Runner-up for the 2007 Main Street Rag Poetry Book Award), *Soledad* (Main Street Rag, 2014) and the unserious *Yodeling Fungus* (Old Mountain Press, 2010). As the convener of the Friday Noon Poets of Chapel Hill he was coeditor of *Always on Friday*, a collection of that group's poems. Dave and his wife Doris live in Cary, North Carolina.

www.ingramcontent.com/pod-product-compliance
Lightning Source LLC
LaVergne TN
LVHW041557070426
835507LV00011B/1138